Delicious B
Bliss Recipes
Special Burgers For The Whole Family

Contents

Introduction 5

    Classic Cheeseburger 9

    Veggie Burger 11

    Chicken Burgers 15

    Beef and Blue Cheese Burgers 17

    Mushroom Burger 20

    Beet Beef Burger 22

    Salmon Burger 25

    Stuffed Burgers with Fried Shallots 28

    Kimchi Burgers 31

    Ginger Pork Burgers 33

    Sausage Burgers 35

    Lamb Burger 37

    BBQ Sauce Burgers Mix 40

    Beef and Mozzarella Burgers 43

    Kidney Bean Burgers 46

    Shrimp Burgers 49

    Turkey Burgers 52

    Pizza Burger 55

Chickpeas Burgers 58

Salmon and Feta Burgers 61

Bacon Cheeseburger 64

Different Egg Burgers 67

Crab Burgers 69

Teriyaki Burgers 72

Pineapple Burgers 74

Bison Burger 76

Honey Beef Burgers 79

Ramen Burgers 81

Cheesy Jalapeno Burgers 84

Lettuce Burgers 86

Black Bean Burgers 89

Quesadilla Burgers 92

Chicken and Cheese Burgers 95

Duck Burgers 98

Tuna Burgers 101

Elegant Burgers 104

Ostrich Burgers 107

Eggplant Burgers 109

Buffalo Burger 112

Eggplant and Zucchini Burgers 115

Potato Burgers 117

Fish Tartar Burgers 119

Cauliflower Burgers 122

Rabbit Burgers 124

Goose Burgers 127

Shrimp and Parsley Mayonnaise Burger 129

Wild Boar Burger 132

Ginger Duck Burger 134

Venison Cheeseburgers 136

Tilapia Burgers 139

Conclusion 142

Introduction

People all over the world consider them a true " culinary treasure". It's the go-to meal when you don't have too much time to cook and eat, it's easy to make and it can taste divine. Yes, you are right: we are talking about burgers. This meal has gained so much popularity all over the world. Food critics search all over for the best recipes, people take photos of them when they order them at restaurants and the whole world has gone crazy over them.

Burgers are an easy and tasty option for everybody. It doesn't matter where you are. You will always find a place where they sell some delicious burgers.

But what happens when you don't have time to go out and get a burger? Well, you can make them at home. That's why we are here today! We bring to you an amazing burger cookbook which will allow you to prepare some special and delicious burgers in the comfort of your own home.

Before preparing the burgers, you might find useful to pay attention to some aspects. First of all, if you are preparing a meat burger, you should make sure you use lean minced meat if you want your burgers to be juicy enough. Beef burgers are classic ones, but these days you can make chicken burgers, lamb, fish, rabbit, seafood, venison or ostrich ones. Just check our recipes and learn how to make all these burgers plus some tasty vegetable ones.

Also, you should pay attention to your flavoring. Use spring onions, garlic, different spices and herbs and make sure you don't forget salt and pepper. We bring through our collection many flavoring options.

Make sure you shape your burgers correctly. Make them really flat before you cook them in order to obtain juicy burgers.

Another aspect you should keep in mind when making burgers at home is the fact that you should keep your patties in the fridge or freezer before cooking them. This allows your burgers to maintain their flavors and shape while cooking.

Make sure you always follow cooking instructions. Don't cook your burgers more than 6 minutes on each side for medium ones or 8 minutes on each side for well-done burgers. This is a very important tip you should consider.

Last but not least, make sure you toast your buns before assembling the burgers. This step is important because it prevents the sauces you use from sinking into the bread. Also, the texture is crisp and nice and you will be able to enjoy a marvelous burger.

Now that you have all these information, it's time to skip to the good part. Let's discover together the best and most delightful burger recipes. Let's enjoy great flavors, textures and tastes. Check out our 50 burger recipes right away and enjoy them all!

Classic Cheeseburger

This classic cheeseburger tastes really incredible!

Serving size: 4

Cooking time: 12 minutes

Ingredients:

- 1 and 1/2 pound lean beef meat, ground
- salt and black pepper to taste
- 4 cheddar cheese slices

- 4 burger buns, halved
- 4 lettuce leaves
- 8 dill pickle slices
- 8 tomato slices
- 2 tablespoons ketchup
- 2 tablespoons mustard
- 2 tablespoons mayonnaise

Instructions:

1. Combine the meat with salt and pepper, stir and shape 4 patties out of this mix.
2. Place patties on preheated kitchen grill and cook them over medium high heat for 5 minutes on each side.
3. Divide the cheddar into each burger, cook for 2 minutes more and take off the heat.
4. Toast the burger bun halves for 1 minute and spread the mayonnaise, ketchup and mustard on each.
5. Divide the lettuce into 4 burger bun halves.
6. Divide the patties, tomato slices and pickle slices, top with the remaining 4 burger bun halves and serve

Veggie Burger

These ultimate veggie burgers are the best! Try them right away!

Serving size: 4

Cooking time: 1 hour and 30 minutes

Ingredients:

- 4 cups water
- 1 tablespoon salt+ a pinch

- 1/3 cup barley
- 1 bay leaf
- 1 pound button mushrooms, quartered
- 2 tablespoons tamari sauce
- 5 tablespoons olive oil
- black pepper to taste
- 1 garlic head, halved crosswise
- 2 carrots, peeled and shredded
- 2 beets, peeled and shredded
- 1 teaspoon smoked paprika
- 1 teaspoon cumin, ground
- 15 ounces canned chickpeas, drained and rinsed
- 1/2 cup panko breadcrumbs
- 1/4 cup walnuts, chopped
- 1 tablespoon mustard
- 4 burger buns, halved and toasted
- 4 butter lettuce leaves
- 1 red onion, sliced
- 4 tomato slices

Instructions:

1. Put the water and the salt in a pan, bring to a boil over medium high heat, stir, add bay leaf and

barley, stir, reduce heat to medium and boil for 30 minutes.
2. Drain the barley, transfer it to a bowl and cool down for 15 minutes.
3. Spread the mushrooms on a lined baking sheet, add tamari sauce, 2 tbsp. oil, some salt and pepper and toss.
4. Place the garlic on an aluminum foil, drizzle ½ tablespoon of oil, wrap foil and place it next to the mushrooms.
5. Roast mushrooms and garlic in preheated oven at 400 degrees F for 40 minutes, cool everything down for 10 minutes, unwrap the garlic and squeeze the flesh into a bowl.
6. Transfer barley to food processor, pulse well, transfer to a bowl and combine with paprika, cumin, beets, and carrots.
7. Put the mushrooms in the food processor, pulse well and transfer to the bowl with the barley mix.
8. Put chickpeas and garlic in the food processor, pulse well and also add to the bowl with the barley mix.
9. Add panko, mustard and walnuts, stir really well and shape 8 patties out of this mix.

10. Heat up a pan with the rest of the oil over medium high heat, add the patties, cook them for 2 minutes on each side and transfer them to a baking sheet.
11. Bake in preheated oven at 400 degrees F for 10 minutes.
12. Divide the lettuce, red onion slices and tomato slices into 4 burger bun halves, divide 2 patties on each, top with the remaining burger bun halves and serve.

Chicken Burgers

We think your kids will like something like this!

Serving size: 6

Cooking time: 10 minutes

Ingredients:

- 1 pound chicken meat, ground
- salt and black pepper to taste
- 1/2 cup milk

- 1/4 cup green onions, chopped
- 1/3 cup breadcrumbs
- 1 teaspoon Worcestershire sauce
- 6 tomato slices
- 6 cucumber slices
- 6 lettuce leaves
- 3 tablespoons mayonnaise
- 6 burger buns, halves

Instructions:

1. In a bowl, combine chicken with breadcrumbs, salt, pepper, milk, green onions and Worcestershire sauce, stir well and shape 6 patties out of this mix.
2. Place burgers on preheated kitchen grill and cook over medium high heat for 5 minutes on each side.
3. Spread the mayonnaise on each burger bun half.
4. Divide the chicken burgers into half of the burger bun halves, also divide the lettuce leaves, tomato slices and cucumber slices, top with the other burger bun halves and serve.

Beef and Blue Cheese Burgers

These are some elegant and special burgers!

Serving size: 2

Cooking time: 20 minutes

Ingredients:

for the burgers:

- 14 ounces deboned rib steak, ground
- 2 teaspoons olive oil

- salt and black pepper to taste

for the sauce:

- 4 tablespoons mayonnaise
- 1/4 teaspoon onion powder
- 1/4 teaspoon garlic powder
- 1/2 teaspoon smoked paprika

for the bacon:

- 4 bacon slices
- 2 teaspoons maple syrup
- 1 teaspoon brown sugar

other ingredients:

- 2 cheddar cheese slices
- 2 ounces blue cheese, grated
- 2 burger buns, halved and toasted
- 2 dill pickles, sliced
- 1 red onion, sliced

Instructions:

1. Combine meat with salt and pepper, stir, shape 2 patties out of this mix and keep in the fridge for 1 hour.
2. In a bowl, combine the mayonnaise with garlic powder, onion powder and smoked paprika, stir well and leave aside for now.
3. Heat up a pan over medium high heat, add bacon and cook for 2 minutes on each side.
4. Add sugar and maple syrup, toss, reduce heat, caramelize bacon for 2-3 minutes more and transfer to a plate.
5. Heat up your kitchen grill over medium high heat, add the burger patties, brush them with the oil and cook for 5-6 minutes on each side.
6. Top each burger with a cheddar cheese, blue cheese and 2 bacon slices, cook for 1 more minutes and divide into 2 burger bun halves.
7. Divide pickles and red onion slices, drizzle the mayonnaise sauce, top with the other 2 burger bun halves and serve.

Mushroom Burger

It tastes even better that meat burgers! Try it soon!

Serving size: 4

Cooking time: 12 minutes

Ingredients:

- 4 portobello mushroom caps
- 2 tablespoons olive oil
- 2 tablespoons balsamic vinegar

- 2 tablespoons tamari sauce
- salt and black pepper to taste
- 4 burger buns, halved and toasted
- 4 lettuce leaves
- 4 tomato slices
- 1 red onion, sliced
- 2 tablespoons ketchup
- 2 tablespoons mayonnaise

Instructions:

1. In a bowl, combine the mushroom caps with oil, vinegar, salt, pepper and tamari sauce, toss well and leave aside for 10 minutes.
2. Place mushroom caps on preheated kitchen grill and cook for 6 minutes on each side.
3. Spread the ketchup and mayonnaise on each burger bun half, divide the mushroom burgers into 4 of them, also divide the lettuce leaves, tomato slices and red onion, top with the other 4 burger bun halves and serve.

Beet Beef Burger

These burgers are simply divine!

Serving size: 4

Cooking time: 10 minutes

Ingredients:

- 1 pound beef meat, ground
- 1 red onion, grated
- salt and black pepper to taste

- 2 tablespoons olive oil
- 4 cheddar cheese slices
- 3 tablespoons mayonnaise
- 4 burger buns, halved and toasted
- 4 lettuce leaves

for the beet relish:

- 1 cup beets, cooked and cubed
- 1 tablespoon red onion, chopped
- 2 tablespoons gherkins, chopped

Instructions:

1. In a bowl, combine beets with gherkins and 1 tablespoon red onion and stir well.
2. In a bowl, combine the meat with grated red onion, salt and pepper, stir well and shape 4 patties out of this mix.
3. Heat up a pan with the oil over medium high heat, add the patties, cook for 3 minutes on each side, divide the cheese slices on each, cook for 2-3 minutes more and take off the heat.
4. Spread each burger bun in half with the mayonnaise, then divide the lettuce, then the

burgers and the beets relish, top with the other burger bun halves and serve.

Salmon Burger

This smoked salmon burger is pretty good! Make it right away!

Serving size: 4

Cooking time: 10 minutes

Ingredients:

- 10 ounces wild salmon fillets, boneless, skinless and chopped

- 4 ounces smoked salmon, boneless, skinless and chopped
- 3 garlic cloves, minced
- 1 yellow onion, chopped
- salt and black pepper to taste
- 1/2 cup panko breadcrumbs
- 4 teaspoons mustard
- 3 tablespoons dill, chopped
- 2 tablespoons lemon juice
- 1 teaspoon hot sauce
- 1/2 cup Greek yogurt
- 2 teaspoons capers, drained and chopped
- 2 tablespoons olive oil
- cooking spray
- 3 burger buns, halved
- 2 cups spring lettuce, torn
- 2 tomatoes, sliced
- 1/2 red onion, sliced

Instructions:

1. In a food processor, combine wild salmon with smoked one, yellow onion, 2 garlic cloves, 1 tablespoon dill, panko, 2 teaspoons mustard, 1

tablespoon lemon juice, olive oil, salt, pepper and hot sauce and pulse well.
2. Shape 4 patties out of this mix and keep them in the fridge for 1 hour.
3. In a bowl, mix your with capers, the rest of the garlic, dill, mustard, lemon juice, salt and pepper, stir well and keep in the fridge for now.
4. Heat up your kitchen grill over medium high heat, grease it with cooking spray, place burgers, cook for 5-6 minutes on each side and transfer them to a plate.
5. Spread the yogurt mix on each burger bun half, divide the lettuce, tomatoes, red onion and patties on half of them, top with the remaining burger bun halves and serve.

Stuffed Burgers with Fried Shallots

The flavors and taste are so unique! These burgers are so good!

Serving size: 4

Cooking time: 20 minutes

Ingredients:

- 8 cups green cabbage, shredded
- salt and black pepper to taste

- 1 cup white vinegar
- 1 tablespoon sugar
- 2 tablespoons mustard seeds
- 3 tablespoons olive oil
- 5 shallots, thinly sliced
- 1/4 cup white flour
- 1 and 1/2 pound beef meat, ground
- 1 teaspoon garlic powder
- 1 teaspoon onion powder
- 1 teaspoon sweet paprika
- 1 tablespoon Worcestershire sauce
- 6 ounces cheddar cheese, shredded
- 2 cups arugula
- 4 burger buns, halved and toasted

Instructions:

1. In a bowl, mix cabbage with salt, stir well and leave aside for 3-4 minutes.
2. Drain the excess water, transfer the cabbage to another bowl, add vinegar, sugar, mustard seeds, 1 cup water and salt to taste, stir well and leave aside for 2 hours.

3. Heat up a pan with the oil over medium high heat, add shallots mixed with the flour, stir, cook for 10 minutes and transfer to a plate.
4. In a bowl, combine the meat with onion powder, garlic powder, paprika, Worcestershire sauce, salt and pepper, stir well and shape 8 patties out of this mix.
5. Press the shredded cheese into 4 patties, place the other 4 patties on top and seal the edges.
6. Place the patties on preheated kitchen grill and cook over medium high heat for 3-4 minutes one on each side.
7. Divide the arugula in half the burger bun halves, divide the burgers on them, drain the cabbage and mound on top of the burgers, top with shallots and the rest of the burger bun halves and serve.

Kimchi Burgers

These bacon and kimchi burgers taste so intense! Everyone will love them!

Serving size: 4

Cooking time: 10 minutes

Ingredients:

- 1/4 cup ketchup
- 1/4 cup mayonnaise

- 1/4 cup chili sauce
- 1 and 1/2 pound beef chuck meat, ground
- 4 bacon slices
- salt and black pepper to taste
- 4 burger buns, halved
- 4 cheddar cheese slices
- 1 cup kimchi cabbage, drained and chopped

Instructions:

1. In a bowl, mix chili sauce with ketchup and mayonnaise, whisk and leave aside.
2. Place bacon on preheated kitchen grill, cook over medium high heat for 2-3 minutes one each side and transfer to a plate.
3. Combine beef meat with salt and pepper, stir and shape 4 patties.
4. Place burgers on preheated grill and cook over medium high heat for 2 minutes on each side.
5. Divide the cheese into each burger, cook for 2 minutes more and take off the heat.
6. Spread the chili mayonnaise mix on each burger bun half, divide the burgers and bacon on half of them, divide the kimchi over the burgers, top with the other burger bun halves and serve.

Ginger Pork Burgers

These flavored and textured burgers are so good!

Serving size: 4

Cooking time: 10 minutes

Ingredients:

- 1 and 1/2 pound pork meat, ground
- 1 tablespoon ginger, grated
- 2 scallions, sliced

- salt and black pepper to taste
- 1 garlic clove, minced
- 1 and 1/2 teaspoons sesame seed oil
- 2 cups coleslaw mix
- 4 burger buns, halved and toasted
- 2 teaspoons rice vinegar
- 2 tablespoons mayonnaise
- 1 teaspoon soy sauce

Instructions:

1. In a bowl, mix pork with ginger, garlic, scallions, salt, pepper and half of the oil, stir well and shape 4 patties out of this mix.
2. Place burgers on preheated kitchen grill and cook over medium high heat for 4-5 minutes on each side.
3. In a bowl, mix coleslaw with vinegar, soy sauce and the rest of the oil and stir well.
4. Spread the mayonnaise on each burger bun half, divide the burgers into half of the burger bun halves, top each with some coleslaw, top with the other burger bun halves and serve.

Sausage Burgers

These Italian style burgers are tasty and easy to make!

Serving size: 4

Cooking time: 20 minutes

Ingredients:

- 1 pound Italian sausages, casings removed
- 10 ounces baby spinach
- 2 tablespoons olive oil

- 1 teaspoon anchovy paste
- 2 garlic cloves, minced
- salt and black pepper to taste
- 1/4 cup sun dried tomato pesto
- 4 slices provolone cheese
- 4 ciabatta rolls, halved and toasted

Instructions:

1. Put some water in a pan, bring to a boil over medium heat, add baby spinach, cook for 1 minute, drain well and clean the pan.
2. Heat up the pan with the oil over medium high heat, add anchovy paste and garlic, stir for 1 minute, add spinach, salt and pepper, stir again, cook for 1 minute and take off the heat.
3. Shape 4 patties out of the sausage meat, place them on preheated kitchen grill and cook over medium high heat for 2-3 minutes on each side.
4. Top each burger with a slice of cheese, cook for 4-5 minutes more and take off the heat.
5. Spread the pesto on the ciabatta rolls, divide the burgers and the spinach and serve.

Lamb Burger

It's time to try something different and flavored!

Serving size: 2

Cooking time: 30 minutes

Ingredients:

- 1/2 pound lamb meat, minced
- 1 bunch mint, chopped
- 1 garlic clove, chopped

- 1 red onion, thinly sliced
- 2 Turkish rolls, halved and toasted
- 1 cup baby spinach
- 1/3 cup panko breadcrumbs
- 1 pound carrots, peeled and cut into sticks
- 1/3 cup garlic aioli
- salt and black pepper to taste
- 2 and 1/2 tablespoons Mediterranean spice mix

Instructions:

1. Spread the carrots on a lined baking sheet, season with salt and pepper, the Mediterranean mix, drizzle half of the oil, toss well and bake in preheated oven at 400 degrees F for 20 minutes.
2. In a bowl, mix lamb with breadcrumbs, garlic, mint, salt and pepper, stir well and shape 2 patties out of this mix.
3. Place the burgers on preheated kitchen grill and cook over medium high heat, cook for 5-6 minutes on each side and transfer to a plate.
4. Split the burger in half width wise and leave aside.

5. Heat up a pan with the rest of the oil over medium high heat, add onion slices and baby spinach, cook for 5 minutes and take off the heat.
6. Spread the aioli on the Turkish roll halves, divide the burgers, the onion and spinach and serve with carrot sticks on the side.

BBQ Sauce Burgers Mix

The BBQ sauce gives such an intense taste to these burgers!

Serving size: 4

Cooking time: 30 minutes

Ingredients:

- 2 pound beef meat, ground
- salt and black pepper to taste

- 1/4 cup hot sauce
- 1/4 cup beef stock
- 6 tablespoons butter, soft
- 8 slices of bread
- 2 tablespoons olive oil
- 1 pound yellow onion, thinly sliced
- salt and black pepper to taste
- 8 bacon slices
- 1 cup gouda cheese, shredded
- 1/4 cup sweet BBQ sauce

Instructions:

1. Heat up a pan with the oil over medium high heat, add the onion, salt and pepper, stir and cook for 5 minutes.
2. Add stock and hot sauce, stir, cook for 5 more minutes and take off the heat.
3. Spread the butter on each bread slice, place with the other side on preheated kitchen grill, toast over medium high heat for 2 minutes and transfer them to a plate.

4. Add the bacon to the grill, cook for 3-4 minutes on each side, drain excess grease on paper towels and leave aside for now.
5. Season the meat with salt and pepper, shape 4 patties, place them on the grill and cook over medium high heat for 2 minutes on each side.
6. Top each burger with the gouda cheese, cook for 1 minute more and take off the heat.
7. Divide the burgers into 4 slices of bread, top with bacon slices, onion and BBQ sauce, top with the other 4 slices of bread and serve.

Beef and Mozzarella Burgers

Have you tried a mozzarella burger before? Then this is the perfect one for you to try today!

Serving size: 6

Cooking time: 10 minutes

Ingredients:

- 1/2 cup olive oil
- 1 garlic clove, minced

- 2 cups basil leaves
- 1/4 cup almonds, roasted
- 1/4 cup pecorino cheese, grated
- salt and black pepper to taste
- 2 pound beef sirloin, ground
- 6 mozzarella slices
- 6 burger buns, halved
- 2 tomatoes, sliced

Instructions:

1. In a blender, combine the basil with garlic, almonds and the oil and blend well.
2. Add pecorino cheese, salt and pepper, pulse again and transfer to a bowl.
3. In a bowl, combine the meat with 1/4 cup of the basil pesto, salt and pepper, stir and shape 6 patties out of this mix.
4. Place the patties on preheated kitchen grill and cook over medium high heat for 3 minutes.
5. Flip the burgers, top each of them with a mozzarella slice, cook for 3 more minutes and take off the heat.
6. Place the burger bun halves on the grill, toast for 1 minute and transfer them to a plate.

7. Spread the pesto on each burger bun halves, divide the burgers and tomatoes in half of them, top with the other burger bun halves and serve.

Kidney Bean Burgers

Did you know you could make an Indian style burger at home? Well, we'll teach you how to make it!

Serving size: 4

Cooking time: 25 minutes

Ingredients:

- 15 ounces canned kidney beans, drained
- 2 eggs, whisked

- 1/4 cup parmesan, grated
- 1/2 cup parsley, chopped
- salt and black pepper to taste
- 1 teaspoon curry powder
- 1 cup breadcrumbs
- 2 tablespoons olive oil
- 4 burger buns, halved and toasted
- 4 cheddar slices
- 4 lettuce leaves
- 1 red onion, sliced
- 3 tablespoons mayonnaise

Instructions:

1. Put the beans in a bowl and mash them well.
2. Add curry powder, eggs, parsley, parmesan, salt and pepper and breadcrumbs, stir really well, leave aside for 10 minutes and shape 4 patties out of this mix.
3. Heat up a pan with the oil over medium high heat, add patties, cook for 4 minutes on each side, introduce in the oven and bake at 375 degrees F for 15 minutes more.

4. Top each burger with a slice of cheese, leave in the oven for 1-2 minutes more and transfer them to a plate.
5. Spread the mayonnaise on each burger bun half, divide the burger in half of them, also divide the lettuce and onion, top with the other burger bun halves and serve.

Shrimp Burgers

Your family will love these shrimp burgers for sure! Try them right away!

Serving size: 4

Cooking time: 12 minutes

Ingredients:

for the mayonnaise:

- 2 egg yolks

- 1 tablespoon white wine vinegar
- 1 teaspoon mustard
- salt and black pepper to taste
- 1 cup olive oil
- 2 tablespoons parsley, chopped
- 2 teaspoons tarragon, chopped
- 2 tablespoons basil, chopped
- zest and juice of 1/2 lemon

for the burgers:

- 1 pound shrimp, peeled and deveined
- 2 tablespoons shallots, minced
- 2 tablespoons parsley, chopped
- 1 teaspoon old bay seasoning
- 1 garlic clove, minced
- 2 tablespoons olive oil
- 1 head frisée, chopped
- 4 burger buns, halved
- juice of 1/2 lemon
- salt and black pepper to taste

Instructions:

1. Put egg yolks in a bowl, add salt and pepper and vinegar and whisk.
2. Add 1 cup oil gradually whisking with a mixer.
3. Add lemon juice and zest from 1/2 lemon, the mustard, 2 tablespoons parsley, basil and tarragon, whisk well and keep in the fridge for now.
4. Meanwhile, in a food processor, combine the shrimp with shallots, 2 tablespoons parsley, salt, pepper, old bay seasoning and garlic clove and pulse well.
5. Shape 4 patties out of this mix.
6. Heat up a pan with 2 tablespoons oil over medium high heat, add shrimp patties, cook for 4-5 minutes on each side and transfer to a plate.
7. Put burger bun halves in the pan, toast over medium high heat for 1-2 minutes on each side and take off the heat.
8. In a bowl, combine frisée with salt, pepper and lemon juice and stir well.
9. Spread the mayonnaise mix on each burger bun half, divide the burgers into half of them, divide the frisée, top with the other burger bun halves and serve.

Turkey Burgers

Serve these burgers with a lemony aioli sauce and you will have the perfect meal!

Serving size: 6

Cooking time: 30 minutes

Ingredients:

- 8 cups warm water
- 2/3 cup salt

- 1 tablespoon brown sugar
- 1 tablespoon lemon zest
- 3 tablespoons lemon juice
- 2 pounds turkey meat, boneless, skinless and chopped
- 1 and 1/4 cups yellow onion, chopped
- 2 tablespoons jalapeno, chopped
- 3 tablespoons olive oil
- 1 tablespoon oregano, chopped
- 1 tablespoon parsley, chopped
- 2 teaspoons rosemary, chopped
- 6 ounces cheddar cheese, grated
- 1 cup mayonnaise
- 6 tomato slices
- 2 tablespoons BBQ sauce
- 1 and 1/2 cups iceberg lettuce, torn
- 6 burger buns, halved and toasted

Instructions:

1. In a large bowl, combine the meat with warm water, salt, brown sugar and 1 tablespoon lemon juice, toss, cover, chill in the fridge for 1 hour and 30

minutes, drain, rinse meat and transfer it to a clean bowl.

2. In a food processor, combine the onion with garlic and jalapeno and pulse well.
3. Heat up a pan with the oil over medium high heat, add onion mix, stir and cook for 5-6 minutes.
4. Add rosemary, oregano and parsley, stir, cook for 1 more minute, take off the heat and cool down for 20 minutes.
5. In a bowl, combine the mayonnaise with lemon zest, some salt and the rest of the lemon juice, stir well, cover and keep in the fridge until you use it.
6. Put the meat in a food processor, pulse well, transfer to a bowl, add the onions mix, stir well and shape 6 patties out of this mix.
7. Place the burgers on preheated kitchen grill and cook over medium high heat for 6 minutes on each side.
8. Top each burger with some cheese, cook for 2 more minutes and take them off the heat.
9. Spread each burger bun half with the lemony mayonnaise and BBQ sauce, divide the patties into half of the burger bun halves, divide the lettuce and

tomato slices as well, cover with the other burger bun halves and serve.

Pizza Burger

This is something different! These pizza burgers are simply awesome!

Serving size: 4

Cooking time: 25 minutes

Ingredients:

- 1 pound beef meat, ground
- 1/4 cup parsley, chopped

- salt and black pepper to taste
- 2 garlic cloves, minced
- 2 tablespoons olive oil
- 2 and 1/2 cups marinara sauce
- 12 pepperoni slices
- 4 mozzarella slices
- 2 teaspoons garlic powder
- 1 teaspoon Italian seasoning
- 2 tablespoons butter, soft
- 4 burger buns, halved
- 1/4 cup parmesan, grated

Instructions:

1. In a bowl, mix beef with salt, pepper, garlic and parsley, stir well and shape 4 patties out of this mix.
2. Heat up a pan with the oil over medium high heat, add patties, cook for 4 minutes, flip them, pour 2 cups marinara in the pan, reduce heat and simmer for 1-2 minutes more.
3. Top each burger with cheese and pepperoni slices, cover the pan and cook everything for 3-4 minutes more.

4. Brush each burger bun half with the butter, sprinkle garlic powder, Italian seasoning and parmesan all over, arrange on a lined baking sheet and bake in preheated oven at 350 degrees F for 10 minutes.
5. Spread the rest of the marinara sauce on half of the burger bun halves, divide the burgers, top with the other burger bun halves and serve.

Chickpeas Burgers

These veggie burgers are simply perfect!

Serving size: 4

Cooking time: 20 minutes

Ingredients:

- 30 ounces canned chickpeas, drained and rinsed
- 2 garlic cloves, minced
- 1 red onion, chopped

- 1/4 cup parsley leaves
- salt and black pepper to taste
- 4 green onions, chopped
- 1 teaspoon cumin, ground
- 1 teaspoon coriander, ground
- 1/4 cup white flour
- 1/4 cup olive oil
- 1 cup Greek yogurt
- 1 cup cucumber, chopped
- 2 tablespoons dill, chopped
- juice of 1 lemon
- 4 burger buns, toasted and halved
- 4 lettuce leaves
- 4 tomato slices

Instructions:

1. Spread chickpeas on a lined baking sheet and bake in preheated oven at 375 degrees F for 10 minutes.
2. Cool the chickpeas down a bit, transfer to a food processor, add onion, garlic, parsley, green onions, salt, pepper, cumin and coriander and pulse well.
3. Add flour, stir again and shape 4 patties out of this mix.

4. Heat up a pan with the oil over medium high heat, add patties and cook them for 3 minutes on each side.
5. Meanwhile, in a bowl, mix yogurt with cucumber, lemon juice and dill and stir well.
6. Spread the yogurt mix on each burger bun half, divide burgers, lettuce and tomato slices, top with the remaining burger bun halves and serve.

Salmon and Feta Burgers

These Mediterranean style burgers are rich and textured. Try them today!

Serving size: 4

Cooking time: 12 minutes

Ingredients:

- 2 pounds salmon fillets, boneless, skinless and chopped

- 2 tablespoons dill, chopped
- 2 tablespoons chives, chopped
- 1 egg, whisked
- salt and black pepper to taste
- 1/2 teaspoon oregano, dried
- 1 cup Greek yogurt
- 1 cup feta cheese, crumbled
- 1/2 teaspoon lemon zest, grated
- cooking spray
- 1 tablespoon mint, chopped
- 1 garlic clove, minced
- 1 tablespoon lemon juice
- 1 red onion, sliced
- 4 tomato slices
- 4 pitas, toasted and split

Instructions:

1. In a food processor, combine the salmon with the egg, pulse well and transfer to a bowl.
2. Add chives, dill, lemon zest, oregano, salt and pepper, stir and shape 4 patties out of this mix.

3. In a separate bowl, combine the yogurt with feta cheese, garlic, mint, lemon juice, salt and pepper and whisk well.
4. Place the patties on preheated kitchen grill, spray with cooking spray and cook over medium high heat for 4 minutes on each side.
5. Divide the salmon burgers, feta sauce, tomato slices and onion slices into each pita and serve.

Bacon Cheeseburger

These bacon cheeseburgers are so delicious and delicious!

Serving size: 4

Cooking time: 20 minutes

Ingredients:

- 1 egg, whisked
- 1/2 tsp. onion powder
- 1/2 tsp. garlic powder

- 1 tsp. sweet paprika
- 1/4 cup milk
- salt and black pepper to taste
- 1/2 cup white flour
- 2 tbsp. cornstarch
- 1 pound beef meat, ground
- 3/4 cup breadcrumbs
- 3 tbsp. olive oil
- 1 yellow onion, sliced
- 8 bacon slices
- 4 cheddar cheese slices
- 3 tbsp. mayonnaise
- 4 burger buns, halved and toasted

Instructions:

1. In a bowl, combine milk with egg, paprika, onion and garlic powder, salt and pepper and whisk well.
2. In another bowl, combine flour with cornstarch and stir.
3. Put the breadcrumbs in a third bowl.
4. Put the onion slices in flour mix, toss, then dredge in egg and coat in breadcrumbs.

5. Heat up a pan with the oil over medium high heat, add onion slices, fry for 2-3 minutes on each side, transfer to a plate, drain excess grease with paper towels and leave them aside.
6. Heat up a pan over medium high heat, add bacon slices, cook for 3-4 minutes and also transfer to a plate.
7. Shape 4 patties out of the beef mix and season them with salt and pepper.
8. Place the burgers on preheated kitchen grill and cook over medium high heat for 3 minutes on each side.
9. Divide the cheese into each burger, fry for 2 more minutes and take them off the heat.
10. Divide the onion rings into half of the burger bun halves, divide the burgers, spread the mayonnaise and bacon, top with the other burger bun halves and serve.

Different Egg Burgers

These are not some classic burgers! Try them and enjoy!

Serving size: 4

Cooking time: 10 minutes

Ingredients:

- 1 pound beef meat, ground
- 2 tablespoons butter
- salt and black pepper to taste

- 4 cheddar cheese slices
- 4 eggs
- 1 tablespoon sriracha
- 3 tablespoons mayonnaise
- 4 burger buns, halved and toasted
- 4 lettuce leaves
- 8 bacon slices, cooked

Instructions:

1. Shape 4 patties out of the beef mix and season with salt and pepper.
2. Using a glass make 4 holes in the patties.
3. Heat up a pan with the butter over medium high heat, add patties and cook them for 2 minutes.
4. Flip them, crack an egg in each pattie, cover the pan and cook for 5 minutes.
5. Top each burger with a slice of cheese and cook for 1 more minute.
6. In a bowl, combine mayonnaise with sriracha and whisk.
7. Spread the mayonnaise mix on each burger bun half, divide the burgers on half of them, also divide the bacon and lettuce, top with the remaining burger bun halves and serve.

Crab Burgers

These burgers are a great alternative to regular beef ones! They are really good!

Serving size: 4

Cooking time: 10 minutes

Ingredients:

- 1 pound crabmeat, shredded
- 1 and 1/2 teaspoons old bay seasoning

- 1 cup breadcrumbs
- 1 teaspoon hot sauce
- 1 tablespoon mustard
- 2 teaspoons lemon juice
- salt and black pepper to taste
- 2 green onions, chopped
- 1 egg, whisked
- 1/4 cup Greek yogurt
- 2 tablespoons olive oil
- 3 tablespoons mayonnaise
- 4 burger buns, halved and toasted
- 4 red onion slices
- 4 lettuce leaves

Instructions:

1. In a bowl, combine green onions with egg, yogurt, mustard, hot sauce, lemon juice, old bay seasoning, crabmeat, breadcrumbs, salt and pepper, stir well and shape 4 patties out of this mix.
2. Heat up a pan with the oil over medium high heat, add patties, cook for 4-5 minutes on each side and take off the heat.

3. Spread the mayonnaise on each burger bun half, divide the patties on half of the burger bun halves, also divide the red onion and lettuce, top with the remaining burger bun halves and serve.

Teriyaki Burgers

These special burgers will make you ask for more!

Serving size: 4

Cooking time: 10 minutes

Ingredients:

- 2 tablespoons mayonnaise
- 1/2 teaspoon red pepper flakes, crushed
- 1 pound beef meat, ground

- 1/4 cup teriyaki sauce
- 4 cheddar cheese slices
- salt and black pepper to taste
- 4 burger buns, halved and toasted
- 4 pineapple slices
- 4 red onion slices
- 4 tomato slices
- 4 lettuce leaves

Instructions:

1. In a bowl, mix mayonnaise with pepper flakes, stir and leave aside for now.
2. Shape 4 patties out of the beef mix, season with salt and pepper and brush them with Teriyaki sauce.
3. Place the burgers on preheated kitchen grill and cook over medium high heat for 4 minutes on each side.
4. Divide the cheese into each burger, leave it on the grill for 2 more minutes and take them off the heat.
5. Spread the mayonnaise mix on each burger bun half, divide the lettuce leaves, burgers, tomato slices, onion slices and pineapple slices on half of

the burger bun halves, top with the remaining ones and serve.

Pineapple Burgers

These are simply so tasty and easy to make!

Serving size: 4

Cooking time: 10 minutes

Ingredients:

- 1 pound beef meat, ground
- 1 tablespoon Worcestershire sauce
- salt and black pepper to taste

- 1 red onion, sliced
- 8 pineapple rings
- 4 cheddar cheese slices
- 4 romaine lettuce leaves
- 4 burger buns, halved and toasted
- 8 bacon slices, cooked

Instructions:

1. In a bowl, mix beef with Worcestershire sauce, salt and pepper, stir well and shape 4 patties out of this mix.
2. Place the burgers on preheated kitchen grill and cook over medium high heat for 4 minutes on each side.
3. Divide the cheese into each burger, leave it on the grill and cook for 2 more minutes.
4. Place the pineapple and onion slices on the grill and cook them for 3 more minutes.
5. Divide the burgers into half of the burger bun halves, also divide the lettuce, pineapple, onion and bacon, top with the remaining burger bun halves and serve.

Bison Burger

This is an elegant burger you can serve at your next family gathering!

Serving size: 8

Cooking time: 30 minutes

Ingredients:

- 2 pound bison meat, ground
- 1 shallot, chopped

- salt and black pepper to taste
- 1 tablespoon Worcestershire sauce
- 2 garlic cloves, minced
- 2 tablespoons butter
- 1/2 teaspoon coriander, ground
- 1/2 teaspoon mustard, ground
- 2 yellow onions, sliced
- 8 cheddar cheese slices
- 8 burger buns, halved and toasted
- 8 lettuce leaves
- 1/2 cup mayonnaise
- 1 tablespoon mustard
- 1/2 teaspoon oregano, dried

Instructions:

1. In a bowl, combine bison meat with shallot, Worcestershire sauce, salt, pepper, ground mustard, garlic and coriander, stir well and shape 8 patties out of this mix.
2. Heat up a pan with the butter over medium high heat, add onions, stir, cook for 20 minutes and take off the heat.

3. Place the burgers on preheated kitchen grill and cook over medium high heat for 4 minutes on each side.
4. Divide the cheese into each burger, cook for 2 more minutes and take off the heat.
5. Combine mayonnaise with mustard and oregano, whisk and spread this on each burger bun half.
6. Divide the burgers, also divide the onions and lettuce leaves, top with the other burger bun halves and serve.

Honey Beef Burgers

These burgers are really flavored!

Serving size: 4

Cooking time: 10 minutes

Ingredients:

- 1 pound beef meat, ground
- 2 tablespoons sweet chili sauce
- 3 tablespoons olive oil

- salt and black pepper to taste
- 1 tablespoon honey
- juice of 1 lime
- 1 tablespoon Sriracha sauce
- 2 cups cabbage, shredded
- 1/3 cup mayonnaise
- 4 burger buns, halved and toasted

Instructions:

1. Combine beef with salt and pepper, stir and shape 4 patties out of this mix.
2. In a bowl, combine chili sauce with oil, sriracha, lime juice and honey and whisk.
3. In another bowl, combine half of this mix with the mayonnaise and whisk really well.
4. Heat up your kitchen grill over medium high heat, add beef patties, cook for 4 minutes on each side basting them with the chili sauce all the time.
5. Spread the mayonnaise mix on each burger bun half, divide the patties and the cabbage, top with the remaining burger bun halves and serve.

Ramen Burgers

It might sound strange at first, but we can assure you that these burgers taste really good!

Serving size: 4

Cooking time: 25 minutes

Ingredients:

- 8 ounces ramen noodles
- salt and black pepper to taste

- 2 eggs, whisked
- 1 pound beef meat, ground
- 1 jalapeno, chopped
- 1 yellow onion, chopped
- 1 green onion, chopped
- 1/2 teaspoon garlic powder
- 4 cheddar cheese slices
- 1 tomato, sliced
- 4 lettuce leaves
- 3 tablespoons olive oil

Instructions:

1. Put water in a pot, add some salt, bring to a boil over medium high heat, add ramen noodles, cook for 6 minutes, drain, rinse with cold water and put them into a bowl.
2. Add eggs, salt and pepper and stir really well.
3. Heat up a pan with the oil over medium high heat, place 4 mason jar lids into the pan, fill each ring with noodles, press well, cook for 4 minutes on each side and transfer to a plate.
4. Repeat with the remaining noodles to make 8 noodle " bun" halves.

5. In a bowl, combine beef with jalapeno, onion, green onion, garlic powder, salt and pepper, stir well and shape 4 patties out of this mix.
6. Heat up the pan where you made the noodle "buns" over medium high heat, add beef patties, cook for 4 minutes on each side, top each burger with a slice of cheese, cook for 2 more minutes and take off the heat.
7. Divide the burgers into half of the ramen "bun" halves, divide lettuce and tomato slices, top with the other ramen "bun" halves and serve.

Cheesy Jalapeno Burgers

These spicy, cheesy and delicious burgers are the perfect meal for you today!

Serving size: 4

Cooking time: 12 minutes

Ingredients:

- 1 and 1/2 pounds beef meat, ground
- 1/2 cup cheddar cheese, shredded

- 1/2 cup mozzarella cheese, shredded
- 2 jalapenos, chopped
- 4 ounces cream cheese
- salt and black pepper, to taste
- 6 bacon slices, cooked and chopped
- 1/2 teaspoon chili powder
- 4 burger buns, halved and toasted

Instructions:

1. In a bowl, combine cheddar with mozzarella, jalapenos, cream cheese, salt, pepper and bacon and stir well.
2. In another bowl, combine the meat with chili powder, salt and pepper, stir well and shape 8 patties out of this mix.
3. Divide the cheese mix into 4 patties, place the other patties on top and seal edges.
4. Place burgers on preheated kitchen grill and cook over medium high heat for 6 minutes on each side.
5. Divide the burgers into half of the burger bun halves, top with the others and serve.

Lettuce Burgers

Try something different today! Try these lettuce burgers and enjoy them!

Serving size: 4

Cooking time: 20 minutes

Ingredients:

- 1 head iceberg lettuce, sliced into 8 rounds
- 1 red onion, sliced

- 1 pound beef meat, ground
- 4 bacon slices
- salt and black pepper to taste
- 1 tomato, sliced
- 4 cheddar cheese slices
- 3 tablespoons mayonnaise

Instructions:

1. Heat up a pan over medium high heat, add bacon, cook for 2-3 minutes on each side, transfer to a plate and drain excess grease with paper towels.
2. Heat up the pan again over medium high heat, add onion slices, cook for 3 minutes on each side and transfer them to a plate.
3. Combine meat with salt and pepper, stir and shape 4 patties out of this mix.
4. Place the burgers on preheated kitchen grill and cook over medium high heat for 4 minutes on each side.
5. Divide the cheese into each burger, cook for 2 more minutes and take them off the heat.
6. Divide the burgers into 4 iceberg lettuce rounds, also divide the bacon, onion and tomato slices,

drizzle the mayonnaise, top with the other 4 iceberg lettuce rounds and serve.

Black Bean Burgers

It's different but so good! These black beans burgers are perfect!

Serving size: 4

Cooking time: 40 minutes

Ingredients:

- 30 ounces canned black beans, drained
- 4 ounces shiitake mushrooms, chopped

- 1 yellow onion, sliced
- 1 tablespoon olive oil
- salt and black pepper to taste
- 1 avocado, peeled, pitted and chopped
- 1/2 cup old fashioned oats
- 1/2 cup parsley, chopped
- 2 garlic cloves, minced
- 2 teaspoons smoked paprika
- 1 teaspoon cumin, ground
- 1 teaspoon chili powder
- 3 tablespoons vegetable oil
- 4 burger buns, halved and toasted
- 4 lettuce leaves
- 4 tomato slices
- 3 tablespoons mayonnaise

Instructions:

1. Spread the black beans on a lined baking sheet, season with salt and pepper, introduce in preheated oven at 375 degrees F, cook for 10 minutes and transfer them to a bowl.
2. Spread the mushrooms and onions on a lined baking sheet, season with salt and pepper, drizzle the olive

oil, toss, bake at 375 degrees F for 20 minutes and cool them down for 10 minutes.

3. In a food processor, combine the beans with mushrooms and onions, oats, avocado, parsley, garlic, paprika, chili powder, cumin, salt and pepper, blend well, shape 4 patties and keep them in the fridge for 10 minutes.
4. Heat up a pan with the vegetable oil over medium high heat, add patties, cook for 4 minutes on each side and take them off the heat.
5. Spread the mayonnaise on each burger bun half, divide the burgers, also divide the lettuce and tomato slices, top with the other burger bun halves and serve.

Quesadilla Burgers

Try these Mexican style burgers as soon as possible!

Serving size: 6

Cooking time: 30 minutes

Ingredients:

- 2 pounds beef meat, ground
- 1 cup black beans, cooked
- 1 tablespoon coriander, chopped

- 1 tablespoon yellow onion, chopped
- 3 garlic cloves, minced
- 2 tablespoons adobo sauce
- salt and black pepper to taste
- 1 tablespoon cumin, ground
- 6 cheddar cheese slices
- 6 tortillas

for the corn:

1. 4 tablespoons olive oil
2. 1 corn on the cob
3. 1 tablespoon red onion, chopped
4. 2 tablespoons coriander, chopped
5. 2 tablespoons chicken stock
6. 2 tablespoons pineapple juice
7. 1 teaspoon cumin, ground
8. salt and black pepper to taste
9. 1 teaspoon hot sauce

Instructions:

1. Brush the corn with 1 tablespoon oil, place it on preheated kitchen grill, cook for 5 minutes on each

side, transfer to a cutting board, cool down, cut kernels and transfer to a bowl.
2. Add 3 tablespoons oil, 1 tablespoon red onion, 2 tablespoons coriander, chicken stock, pineapple juice, 1 teaspoon cumin, salt, pepper and hot sauce, stir well, cover and leave aside for now.
3. In a bowl, combine beef with 1 tablespoon coriander, black beans, yellow onion, salt, pepper, garlic, adobo sauce and 1 tablespoon cumin, stir well and shape 6 patties out of this mix.
4. Heat up your kitchen grill over medium high heat, add burgers, cook for 5 minutes on each side, add the cheese on top, cook for 2 more minutes and take off the heat.
5. Layer a burger on each tortilla, divide the corn equal on each, fold and roll like a burrito, place them on your preheated grill, cook for 2-3 minutes, cut each in halves and serve.

Chicken and Cheese Burgers

Check out these tasty burgers!

Serving size: 4

Cooking time: 20 minutes

Ingredients:

- 2 chicken breasts, skinless, boneless and cut in 4 pieces
- 1 tablespoon olive oil

- salt and black pepper to taste
- 4 tablespoons piri-piri sauce
- juice of 1/2 lemon
- 4 burger buns, halved
- 8 pieces halloumi cheese
- 1/4 cup green cabbage, shredded
- 2 tablespoons mayonnaise
- 4 tablespoons hummus
- 4 lettuce leaves
- 2 roasted red peppers, sliced

Instructions:

1. Heat up a pan with the oil over medium high heat, add the chicken pieces, season with salt and pepper and cook for 4 minutes on each side.
2. Add piri-piri sauce, half of the lemon juice, toss, cook for 2 minutes more and take off the heat.
3. Heat up another pan over medium high heat, add halloumi, cook for 1 minute on each side and transfer to a plate.
4. In a bowl, combine the cabbage with the rest of the lemon juice and mayonnaise and stir well.

5. Spread the hummus on each burger bun half, divide the lettuce, chicken, haloumi, peppers and the cabbage on half of them, top with the other burger bun halves and serve.

Duck Burgers

These burgers are served with a tasty cherry salsa! The taste is amazing!

Serving size: 2

Cooking time: 2 hours and 20 minutes

Ingredients:

- 3 duck legs
- 1/2 cup cherries, pitted

- 1/2 teaspoon nutmeg, ground
- 1 star anise
- a pinch of salt and black pepper
- 1 egg, whisked
- 1/4 cup breadcrumbs
- 2 burger buns, halved and toasted
- 2 tablespoons olive oil

for the salsa:

- 1/2 cup red onion, chopped
- 1/2 cup cherries, pitted and halved
- 1/2 teaspoon lemon juice
- 1 tablespoon balsamic vinegar
- a pinch of salt and black pepper
- a handful of parsley, chopped

Instructions:

1. In a bowl, combine 1/2 cup cherries with red onion, lemon juice, balsamic vinegar, salt, pepper and the parsley, stir, cover and leave aside in the fridge for now.

2. Place duck legs skin side up, 1/2 cup cherries, star anise, nutmeg, salt and pepper in a pan, toss and bake in preheated oven at 300 degrees F for 2 hours.
3. Take the duck legs out of the oven, cool them down, remove skin, shred finely, transfer to a bowl, add cherries from the pan, breadcrumbs and egg, stir, shape 2 patties out of this mix and keep in the fridge for 1 hour.
4. Heat up a pan with the oil over medium high heat, add duck burgers, cook for 2-3 minutes on each side and take off the heat.
5. Divide the burgers on half of the burger bun halves, divide the cherry salsa on top, top with the remaining burger bun halves and serve.

Tuna Burgers

These tuna burgers go perfect with a cucumber salsa!

Serving size: 2

Cooking time: 6 minutes

Ingredients:

- 1 and 1/2 cups canned tuna in water, drained and flaked
- 2 burger buns, halved

- zest and juice of 1 lime
- 3 tablespoons coriander, chopped
- salt and black pepper to taste
- 3 teaspoons olive oil
- 1 teaspoon sriracha sauce
- 3 tablespoons mayonnaise
- 1 cucumber, cubed
- 2 tomatoes, sliced
- a handful iceberg lettuce, shredded

Instructions:

1. In a bowl, combine tuna with zest and juice of 1/2 lime, half of the coriander, salt, pepper, 1 teaspoon oil, sriracha and 1 tablespoon mayonnaise, stir really well, shape 2 burgers and keep them in the fridge for now.
2. In another bowl, mix cucumber with the rest of the lime juice and zest, coriander, salt and pepper, and stir.
3. Heat up a pan with the rest of the oil over medium high heat, add tuna burgers, cook for 3 minutes on each side and take off the heat.

4. Spread the rest of the mayonnaise on each burger bun half, divide the burgers, the salsa, lettuce and tomatoes, top with the other burger bun halves and serve.

Elegant Burgers

These gourmet burgers are pretty impressive! The taste is awesome for sure!

Serving size: 4

Cooking time: 25 minutes

Ingredients:

- 1 yellow onion, chopped
- 8 ounces beef meat, ground

- 3 teaspoons tabasco sauce
- salt and black pepper to taste
- 1 ounce breadcrumbs
- 1 tomato, sliced
- 1 red onion, sliced
- 1 tablespoon feta cheese, shredded
- a handful rocket leaves
- 4 ciabatta rolls, toasted

for the salsa:

1. 1 small yellow onion, chopped
2. 1/2 tablespoons olive oil
3. 1 green bell pepper, chopped
4. 1/2 cup tomatoes, cubed
5. 1/2 tablespoon lime juice
6. a pinch of salt and black pepper
7. 1/2 teaspoon tabasco sauce
8. 1/2 tablespoon coriander, chopped

Instructions:

1. Heat up a pan with the oil over medium high heat, add 1 small yellow onion, stir and cook for 4 minutes.

2. Add bell pepper, tomato, 1/2 tablespoon lime juice, salt, pepper, 1/2 teaspoon tabasco sauce and 1/2 tablespoon coriander, stir, cook for 4-5 minutes more, take off the heat, transfer to a bowl and leave aside.
3. In a bowl, mix beef with salt, pepper, 3 teaspoons tabasco, breadcrumbs and 1 yellow onion, stir and shape 4 patties out of this mix.
4. Place the burgers on preheated kitchen grill and cook over medium high heat for 5 minutes on each side.
5. Divide burgers into ciabatta rolls, also divide the salsa, tomato slices, red onion slices, feta cheese and rocket leaves and serve.

Ostrich Burgers

We know for sure you will enjoy these special and different burgers!

Serving size: 4

Cooking time: 15 minutes

Ingredients:

- 1 pound ostrich, ground
- 1 teaspoon olive oil

- salt and black pepper to taste
- 2 tablespoons yellow onion, chopped
- 1 garlic clove, minced
- 4 burger buns, halved and toasted
- 4 lettuce leaves
- 4 tomato slices

Instructions:

1. Heat up a pan with the oil over medium high heat, add onion and garlic, stir, cook for 5 minutes and take off the heat.
2. In a bowl, mix ostrich meat with onion and garlic, salt and pepper, stir and shape 4 patties out of this mix.
3. Place the burgers on preheated kitchen grill and cook over medium high heat for 5 minutes on each side.
4. Divide the lettuce into 4 burger bun halves, also divide the burgers, top with tomato slices and the rest of the burger bun halves and serve.

Eggplant Burgers

Here's another great veggie burger you should try!

Serving size: 4

Cooking time: 50 minutes

Ingredients:

- 2 eggplants, pricked with a fork
- 1 teaspoon garlic powder
- 1 yellow onion, sliced

- 1 tablespoon olive oil
- salt and black pepper to taste
- 2 teaspoons smoked paprika
- 1 teaspoon oregano, dried
- 1 tablespoon sugar
- 5 tablespoons BBQ sauce
- 1 and 1/2 cups canned black beans, drained
- 4 burger buns, halved and toasted
- 4 lettuce leaves

Instructions:

1. Put the eggplants on preheated kitchen grill and cook them over medium high heat for 30 minutes.
2. Heat up a pan with the oil over medium high heat, add onion, stir and fry for 10 minutes.
3. Scoop flesh from eggplants and transfer them to the pan with the onions.
4. Also add garlic powder, paprika, sugar, oregano, salt and pepper, BBQ sauce and black beans.
5. Toss well and bake in preheated oven at 400 degrees F for 15 minutes.

6. Divide the lettuce into 4 burger bun halves, divide the eggplant mix into 4 parts, top with the other burger bun halves and serve.

Buffalo Burger

If you are looking for different burger ideas, then this is the right place for you! Here's a special burger recipe!

Serving size: 2

Cooking time: 30 minutes

Ingredients:

- 1 yellow onion, sliced
- 2 tablespoons butter

- 1/2 pound buffalo meat, ground
- salt and black pepper to taste
- 1/4 teaspoon sweet paprika
- 1/4 teaspoon onion powder
- 2 burger buns, halved and toasted
- 2 tablespoons mayonnaise
- 1/4 cup blue cheese, crumbled
- 2 tablespoons hot sauce
- 2 lettuce leaves

Instructions:

1. Heat up a pan with the butter over medium high heat, add onions, stir and sauté for 20 minutes.
2. In a bowl, combine meat with salt, pepper, paprika and onion powder, stir and shape 2 patties out of this mix.
3. Place burger on preheated kitchen grill and cook over medium high heat for 5 minutes on each side.
4. Top each burger with blue cheese, leave on the grill for 2 more minutes and take off the heat.
5. Spread the mayonnaise and hot sauce on each burger bun half, divide the lettuce, burgers and

onions, top with the other burger bun halves and serve.

Eggplant and Zucchini Burgers

If you are searching for a vegetarian burger, then you should consider try this one!

Serving size: 4

Cooking time: 20 minutes

Ingredients:

- 1 eggplant, sliced
- 1 zucchini, sliced

- 1 red onion, sliced
- 1 red bell pepper, cut into 4 pieces
- 3 tablespoons olive oil
- salt and black pepper to taste
- 2 teaspoons thyme leaves
- 1/2 bunch basil, chopped
- 2 tomatoes, chopped
- 4 tablespoons hummus
- 2 teaspoons red wine vinegar
- 4 ciabatta buns, toasted
- a handful rocket

Instructions:

1. Spread the eggplant, zucchini, onion and bell pepper on a lined baking sheet, add half of the oil, salt, pepper and thyme, toss and roast in preheated oven at 400 degrees F for 15 minutes.
2. In a bowl, mix tomato with salt, pepper, vinegar, basil and the rest of the oil and toss.
3. Spread the hummus on each ciabatta bun base, divide the rocket, divide the roasted veggies, then add tomato salsa on each, top with the bun tops and serve.

Potato Burgers

We offer you so many different and special burger ideas. This will soon become your favorite one.

Serving size: 4

Cooking time: 2 hours and 20 minutes

Ingredients:

- 4 large gold potatoes, brushed
- salt and black pepper to taste

- 2 tablespoons olive oil
- 2 yellow onions, sliced
- 2 tablespoons butter
- 4 cheddar cheese sliced
- 1 pound beef meat, ground and shaped into 4 patties
- 4 lettuce leaves
- 4 tomato slices

Instructions:

1. Place the potatoes in a baking tray, prick them with a fork, season with salt and pepper, drizzle half of the oil, rub and bake in preheated oven at 400 degrees F for 2 hours.
2. Heat up a pan with the rest of the oil over medium high heat, add onion, stir and sauté for 10 minutes.
3. Place the burgers on preheated kitchen grill and cook for 3 minutes on each side.
4. Add the cheese, leave the burgers on the grill for 2 more minutes and take them off the heat.
5. Cut the potatoes in half horizontally, spread the butter on each half, divide the lettuce, tomato, onions and burgers on half of the potato halves, top with the other halves and serve.

Fish Tartar Burgers

This is a simple but really delicious burger idea!

Serving size: 4

Cooking time: 8 minutes

Ingredients:

- 2 eggs, whisked
- 1/2 cup white flour
- 1 cup breadcrumbs

- juice and zest of 1 lemon
- 2 and 1/2 tablespoons dill, chopped
- 4 cod fillets, boneless and skinless
- 2/3 cup mayonnaise
- salt and black pepper to taste
- 2 gherkins, chopped
- 1 tablespoon capers, chopped
- 3 tablespoons olive oil
- 4 bread rolls, halved and toasted
- 1 cup coleslaw mix

Instructions:

1. Put the flour in a bowl, the eggs in another one and combine breadcrumbs with lemon zest and 2 tablespoons dill in a third one.
2. Season fish with salt and pepper, coat in flour, then dredge in egg and then in breadcrumbs mix.
3. In a bowl, combine mayonnaise with the rest of the dill, gherkin, capers and the lemon juice and whisk well.
4. Heat up a pan with the oil over medium high heat, add fish fillets, cook for 3-4 minutes on each side and transfer to a plate.

5. In a bowl, mix coleslaw with 1/3 of the mayonnaise mix and stir well.
6. Spread this mix on bread roll bases, then add the fish, drizzle the mayonnaise mix, top with the bread roll tops and serve.

Cauliflower Burgers

It's one of our favorite burger ideas!

Serving size: 2

Cooking time: 25 minutes

Ingredients:

- 1 small cauliflower
- 2 and 1/2 tablespoons hot chili sauce
- 1 cup Greek yogurt

- 2 burger buns, halved and toasted
- 4 lettuce leaves
- 1 tablespoon olive oil
- salt and black pepper to taste
- 1 teaspoon oregano, dried
- 1 teaspoon garlic powder

Instructions:

1. Trim the cauliflower, cut a slice from the middle and then halve this to make 2 cauliflower burgers.
2. Heat up a pan with the oil over medium high heat, add cauliflower burgers, season with salt and pepper and cook for 5 minutes on each side.
3. Brush the burgers with the chili sauce and roast in preheated oven at 400 degrees F for 15 minutes.
4. Meanwhile, combine yogurt with garlic powder and oregano and stir well.
5. Spread the yogurt mix on each burger bun in half, divide the cauliflower burgers into half of the burger bun halves, divide the lettuce, top with the rest of the burger bun halves and serve.

Rabbit Burgers

These rabbit burgers are incredible! They taste really great!

Serving size: 8

Cooking time: 1 hour and 15 minutes

Ingredients:

- 8 tomatoes, halved
- 2 tablespoons olive oil
- a bunch watercress

- 6 tablespoons mayonnaise
- salt and black pepper to taste
- 1 cup blue cheese, shredded
- 8 burger buns, halved and toasted

for the burgers:

- 1 and 1/2 pound rabbit meat, minced
- 1 pound pork meat, minced
- 1/2 bunch parsley, chopped
- 1/2 bunch thyme, chopped
- 1 garlic clove, crushed
- 1/2 cup breadcrumbs
- salt and black pepper to taste

Instructions:

1. Place the tomato halves on a lined baking sheet, season with salt and pepper, drizzle the oil and roast in preheated oven at 375 degrees F for 1 hour.
2. Chop half of the watercress and combine it in a bowl with the mayonnaise.
3. In a bowl, mix rabbit meat with pork meat, parsley, thyme, garlic, breadcrumbs, salt and pepper, stir and shape 8 patties out of this mix.

4. Place the burgers on preheated kitchen grill and cook over medium high heat for 4 minutes on each side.
5. Top each burger with some blue cheese, leave on the grill for one more minute and take them off the heat.
6. Divide the remaining watercress into half of the burger bun halves, then spread some of the mayonnaise on them, then divide the burgers, then add 2 tomato halves on each burger, top with the rest of the burger bun halves and serve.

Goose Burgers

You will be impressed with the amazing taste!

Serving size: 4

Cooking time: 10 minutes

Ingredients:

- 1 pound goose breast, boneless, skinless and ground
- salt and black pepper to taste
- 1/3 cup Italian dressing

- 1 cup white flour
- 1/4 teaspoon garlic powder
- 5 burger buns, halved and toasted
- 3 tablespoons olive oil
- 4 lettuce leaves
- 3 tablespoons mayonnaise

Instructions:

1. In a bowl, mix goose with salt, pepper and Italian dressing, stir well and keep in the fridge for 1 hour.
2. In a bowl, mix flour with salt, pepper and garlic powder and stir well.
3. Make 4 patties out of the goose mix and dredge each in flour mix.
4. Heat up a pan with the oil over medium high heat, add burgers, cook for 5 minutes on each side and take off the heat.
5. Spread the mayonnaise on each burger bun half, divide the lettuce and the burgers on half of them, top with the remaining burger bun halves and serve.

Shrimp and Parsley Mayonnaise Burger

The combination is simply perfect! If you like seafood, then you will love this burger!

Serving size: 4

Cooking time: 12 minutes

Ingredients:

- 2 tablespoons mayonnaise

- 1 tablespoon parsley, chopped
- 1 teaspoon tabasco sauce
- a pinch of salt and black pepper

for the shrimp:

- 1 pound shrimp, peeled and deveined
- 2 tablespoons olive oil
- 1 shallot, chopped
- 1 yellow bell pepper, chopped
- 2 garlic cloves, minced
- 1 teaspoon chili powder
- 1 teaspoon sweet paprika
- 2 teaspoons mustard, ground
- 1 tablespoon lemon juice
- 1/2 tablespoons Worcestershire sauce
- salt and black pepper to taste

to assemble:

- 4 burger buns, halved and toasted
- 1 tomato, sliced
- 4 lettuce leaves

Instructions:

1. In a bowl, mix mayonnaise with parsley, tabasco, salt and pepper, whisk and keep in the fridge for now.
2. Heat up a pan with the oil over medium high heat, add shallot and bell pepper, stir and cook for 2-3 minutes.
3. Add shrimp, stir and sauté for 2 more minutes.
4. Add garlic, chili powder, paprika, ground mustard, lemon juice, Worcestershire sauce, salt and pepper, stir and cook everything for 4-5 minutes more.
5. Spread the mayonnaise on each burger bun half, divide the lettuce, tomato slices and shrimp on half of them, top with the other burger bun halves and serve.

Wild Boar Burger

Were you looking for a really special, flavored and rich burger? This is the best one!

Serving size: 4

Cooking time: 10 minutes

Ingredients:

- 1 pound wild boar belly, ground
- 1 tablespoon Worcestershire sauce

- 1 tablespoon chili sauce
- 1 tablespoon tomato sauce
- 2 shallots, sliced
- salt and black pepper to taste
- 4 burger buns, halved and toasted
- 2 tablespoons olive oil
- 2 apples, sliced
- 2 tablespoons blue cheese, shredded
- 1 small bunch watercress

Instructions:

1. In a bowl, combine the meat with Worcestershire sauce, chili sauce, shallots, tomato sauce, salt and pepper, stir and shape 4 burgers out of this mix.
2. Heat up a pan with the oil over medium high heat, add burgers, cook for 4 minutes on each side, divide the cheese on each, cook for 2 more minutes and take off the heat.
3. Divide the burgers into half of the burger bun halves, also divide the watercress and apple slices, top with the remaining burger bun halves and serve.

Ginger Duck Burger

Get all the ingredients you need and make this awesome burger!

Serving size: 5

Cooking time: 10 minutes

Ingredients:

- 2 duck breasts, skinless and boneless
- 2 white bread slices, chopped

- 1 yellow onion, chopped
- 1/2 cup parsley, chopped
- 1 teaspoon ginger, grated
- salt and black pepper to taste
- 1/2 teaspoon chili flakes, crushed
- 1 egg, whisked
- 1 tablespoon olive oil
- 10 mini brioche burger rolls, halved
- 3 tablespoons hoisin sauce
- 1 cup kale, chopped

Instructions:

1. Put the meat in a food processor and pulse well.
2. Add bread, onion, parsley, ginger, salt, pepper, chili flakes and the egg, pulse well and shape 10 small burgers out of this mix.
3. Heat up a pan with the oil over medium high heat, add mini burgers, cook for 4-5 minutes on each side and take them off the heat.
4. Spread the hoisin sauce on each burger bun half, divide the burgers into half of them, divide the kale, top with the other burger bun halves and serve.

Venison Cheeseburgers

Don't worry! We are sure you will get all the ingredients you need really fast to make this great burger!

Serving size: 4

Cooking time: 35 minutes

Ingredients:

- 1 pound venison meat, minced
- 2 tablespoons olive oil

- 1 yellow onion, chopped
- 1 garlic clove, minced
- 6 sage leaves, chopped
- 1 cup apples, cored and chopped
- salt and black pepper to taste
- 2 tablespoons mustard
- 1 egg yolk
- 1/2 cup breadcrumbs
- 1 cup cheddar cheese, shredded
- 4 burger buns, halved and toasted
- 2 tablespoons mayonnaise
- 4 tomato slices

Instructions:

1. Heat up half of the oil in a pan over medium high heat, add onion, stir and cook for 5 minutes.
2. Add garlic, sage, apple, some salt and pepper, stir, cook for 10 minutes and take off the heat.
3. In a bowl, combine venison with apples and onions mix, add mustard, egg yolk, breadcrumbs, half of the cheese, salt and pepper, stir well and shape 4 patties out of this mix.

4. Heat up a pan with the rest of the oil over medium high heat, add burgers, cook for 4 minutes on each side, add the rest of the cheese on each and introduce in the oven at 400 degrees F for 10 minutes.
5. Spread the mayonnaise on each burger bun half, divide the burgers into half of them, divide the tomato slices and top with the other burger bun halves.

Tilapia Burgers

The taste is fresh and the texture is just perfect!

Serving size: 4

Cooking time: 10 minutes

Ingredients:

for the sauce:

- 1/2 cup mayonnaise
- 2 tablespoons dill pickles, chopped

- 1 tablespoon capers, chopped
- 1 tablespoon lemon juice
- 1 tablespoon white wine vinegar
- 1 teaspoon lemon zest, grated
- 1 teaspoon dill, chopped

for the burgers:

- 1 and 1/2 pounds tilapia fillets, boneless and skinless
- zest of 1 lemon
- salt and black pepper to taste
- 3 tablespoons chives, chopped
- 1 tablespoon mustard
- 1 tablespoon dill, chopped
- 1 tablespoon olive oil
- 4 burger buns, halved and toasted
- 4 lettuce leaves
- 4 tomato slices

Instructions:

1. In a bowl, combine the mayonnaise with dill pickles, capers, lemon juice, vinegar, 1 teaspoon

lemon zest and 1 teaspoon dill, whisk well and keep in the fridge for now.
2. In a food processor, combine tilapia with zest of 1 lemon, salt, pepper, chives, mustard and 1 tablespoon dill, pulse well, shape 4 patties out of this mix and keep them in the fridge for 30 minutes.
3. Heat up a pan with the oil over medium high heat, add tilapia burgers, cook for 4-5 minutes on each side and take them off the heat.
4. Spread the mayonnaise mix on each burger bun half, divide the lettuce, burgers and tomato slices on half of them, top with the remaining burger bun halves and serve.

Conclusion

You found the best burger recipes collection ever available on the market. We searched and brought you the best and most delicious burger recipes. Whether we like it or not or whether we consider them healthy or not, we all have to agree that burgers have gained so much popularity all over the world and that they have become a favorite meal for people all over the world.

They are such a simple option for lunch or dinner, they are perfect for a quick meal at the office and they can even be a good option for a night out.

That is why we thought we could bring to you a burger recipes collection filled with simple and accessible burger recipes that anyone can make in the comfort of their own home. All the recipes you discovered in this special collection are amazing and tasty and we think you should try them all as soon as possible.

So, what are you still waiting for? Gather all the ingredients you need and prepare some special burgers for you and all your loved ones! Enjoy the rich tastes and flavors!

Printed in Great Britain
by Amazon